"I appreciated the unabashed humor, sarcasm, vulnerability, tips and pointers and brilliant story sharing that was used to underscore the importance of appropriately wrapping up a life. *Ghost or Guardian* adds levity to a topic and reality with which we will all grapple someday."

—SHEILA HIGGS BURKHALTER,
MBA, MSED, CPC, ELI-MP

"Straight to the point about modern human death, Cyndy gives invaluable advice for planning your passing well before your final hours. Equal parts laughter and learned wisdom, this guide convinces readers to leave behind much more than headaches. In the end, it's your choice: will you be the Ghost or Guardian?"

—STEPHANIE JOONG, MBA,
WOMEN'S LEADERSHIP AUTHOR
AND CAREER CONSULTANT

"*Ghost or Guardian* is a remarkably thoughtful and thought-provoking book. It masterfully balances a light touch with serious content, ensuring that readers engage deeply with the important task of preparing for their own departure. The practical insights provided are genuinely enlightening, even for an archivist like myself, who frequently navigates the realm of legacy. The book addresses somber and weighty topics with the necessary gravity, offering crucial guidance on matters often left unspoken, and typically realized only in the midst of grief and loss. This work is an invaluable resource for those wishing to ensure their legacy is a blessing rather than a burden to their loved ones."

—DOMINIQUE LUSTER,
CEO AND PRINCIPAL ARCHIVIST,
THE LUSTER COMPANY

PRAISE FOR GHOST OR GUARDIAN

"This book's light and airy, comedic style about the emotionally fraught process of dying and its aftermath, makes it useful and hilarious at the same time. Although it does sometimes bring us up short when considering our own demise, it offers solid advice about how to make our death a little less painful to those we leave behind. The suggestions are eminently practical and the delivery left me alternately chuckling and teary eyed page after page."

—MARYELLEN FUNARO, MS
LIBRARY AND INFORMATION SCIENCE

"Cyndy makes the discussions of passing away actually interesting for the passers and the survivors. Quite insightful and full of good common sense. Amusing style keeps you turning pages."

—DICK MUELLER,
COLONEL, AIR FORCE RETIRED

Dedicated to our future.
Harper, Griffin, and Bryson

Copyright © 2024
by Hunter Street Press
All rights reserved.

Hunter Street
Press

ISBN: 978-1-7372751-5-2

Cover design and interior formatting by
TeaBerryCreative.com

GHOST or GUARDIAN

A Guidebook for the Pre-Dead

Do these things before you die
so your heirs won't hate you later

CYNDY WULFSBERG

TABLE OF CONTENTS

Praise for Ghost or Guardian i
Introduction............................... xi
Ghost or Guardian........................... xv

1: URGENT! URGENT! You are dead. 1
  Keys 2
  The Body 7
  Remaining Living Things...................... 13
    Pets.................................. 13
    Plants................................ 19
    Stowaways 21
  Undertakers 23
  Your Corpse 30
  Instructions and messages from Beyond............ 36
    Messages about your body 37
    Fireproof safes 43
    Safe deposit boxes and banks............... 44
    Contents of Safe—Documentation—Checklist........... 48
    Document Checklist...................... 50
    This book on your desk 51
  Obituary—Memorial—After-Party Checklist.......... 53
    The Obit.............................. 56
    The Memorial/After Party................. 59
    Memorial Checklist 62
  Mail, Call Forwarding, Email, Social Media 65
    Mail 66

Call forwarding/phones 68
Email and Social Media 71

2: YOUR ESTATE: Now that you are out of the way, there is still a paper trail. 75

Cash 76
Bank Accounts 78
Insurance, Annuities, and IRAs 80
Trusts, Wills and Probate 84
Where you Live: Real Estate 89

3: YOUR STUFF: Instructions for Handling Earthly Belongings 101

Stuff you may not want your kids to see 102
Stuff you don't want anyone to have to sort through . 105
Stuff of value they will accidentally toss if you don't sort it out 106
Stuff of value you should sell because they don't care ... 107
Stuff they will love if you organize it now 109
Stuff they can do, no problem—
leave it to them and don't waste a minute on it 111

4: SPECIAL WARNINGS 115

Stuff that doesn't belong to you 115
Dangers of Storage Units 116

Disclaimer 125
Acknowledgements 127
About the Author 129

INTRODUCTION

Before every child-free vacation, I placed this letter on my desk.

If you are reading this, I am not going to be able to help you with the mess I have left behind. I am so sorry for burdening you with piles of papers, hoarded possessions, and unidentified family photos that could take a lifetime to sort through. You don't have to do it. It is my mess. Do what you need to do to get on with your life. I wish I could be there to watch your story unfold. That would be my greatest joy.

I love you,
Mom

That letter eased my guilt enough that I could leave the kids and minimally acknowledge the chaos left behind. It was really no help to anyone but me, as it relieved my contrition temporarily. I left behind my mess while away and returned to see it still waiting for me.

Then my parents died, and they left me their mess—papers, possessions, and photos. What a dirty trick! Ironically, the more I cleaned up their worldly possessions, the worse my mess became. The only thing that kept me digging out was drafting this book and working on my own legacy problem.

If you feel lousy about your piles of stuff, and the burden that might be left, this book is for you! Read it, follow the steps, and feel confident your friends and family won't curse you when you're gone. If you leave a highlighted copy of this book on your desk, it may even stop the legacy that so often occurs, that of cleaning up for someone else.

The best time to read this book is when you are alive, peppy, and overconfident. The next best time is when you realize you are mortal and had better do something about the challenge at hand. We worry so much about becoming a physical burden on our loved ones, and then neglect to manage the havoc life creates, which will absolutely burden them. If you are dead already (Wow! How did you get a copy?), this can absolutely help your survivors wade through life's leavings and do a better job for the next generation.

You have a choice. You can be a Guardian Angel or a Ghost of Clutter Past. No need to be buried beneath tasks left undone before your physical exit from this earth. Look at the Table of Contents and start somewhere. Do the easy jobs first. Just in case.

GHOST OR GUARDIAN

The process of choosing your preferred post-life status, Ghost of Clutter Past or Guardian Angel, is one that you can make generally for all the people you leave behind, or you can target specific people for special attention. Throughout the book I have referred to the people who remain breathing after you have ceased the effort and will participate in your clean up as heirs, crew, clean-up crew, loved ones, children, family, friends, team, or butler.

All descriptors are meant to give you the idea without attributing responsibility. You can do that if you like, and it may be fun to choose labels of your own for these remaining souls if you don't want to call them by name. Your labels would make it clearer if you are planning to haunt particular individuals or conversely, bless others with your consideration and generosity.

I also refer to your day of departure as your DDay, and do not intend in any way to slight WWII veterans who ascribe a different meaning to the term.

The book is presented in order of typical required action from your physical expiration to the closing of your estate and cessation of all work regarding your existence. Odes of praise can continue but at some celebrated time, the work of your life will be over.

You need not approach your clean up in the order presented. Although this is a guidebook, you are encouraged to find your own way through it, but you will accomplish more if you set a schedule. Maybe every Monday you tackle the job. Maybe you work for an hour each day or plan a time when you lock the door, turn on music everyone else hates and dig into it. Unless you are an unusual human for whom procrastination is not a problem (and someone probably gave you this book, so I don't think so) then pick a chapter and get busy!

Part One
URGENT! URGENT!
You are dead.

Pretend you are going on a long vacation and think of all the preparations you make: the notes you leave, the people who check the house for you, your plans for mail and bills, pets and plants. This section offers suggestions for many of these elements, but undoubtedly you have unique situations and things to consider that are not covered in this book.

Living things are a greater challenge than stashes of inert belongings, no matter how unusual. "Consider the living" is a consistent theme. And not all living things you leave behind are pets. For instance, if your cat routinely stares and scratches at the living room wall, there may be an uninvited guest living in the wall that you should evict. Even if you expect the wall creature to outlive you, you still don't get to ignore it—unless you want it to be a curse and your clean-up crew deserves to discover this on their own.

KEYS

(Touchpads, alarm systems)

Keys are an example of an actual logistical problem your family must cope with while they are struggling with grief. You can help. Can they get to your cooling corpse, or must someone break down the door to reach you? Breaking down the door means that you are already costing your loved ones money and heartache.

While old fashioned keys may not be involved in the touchpad world, if you do have them, make sure several of your responsible crew members have a copy. One should be close by. A neighbor who tends to be home is an excellent choice, and your trusted children should have one too.

Cute exterior key holders have their pitfalls. I had a decorative cement turtle that had a hole in its tail end. I placed this turtle by the edge of a little pond near my back walk. He sat there just as a real turtle might sit. The key was housed in a plastic bag and inserted, colonoscopy style, and rested in his belly. When the key was finally needed, several feet of snow and natural corrosion had rendered it useless. The effort to find the useless key constituted a mild curse. The corroded key resulted in a broken window.

If you must break a window, be sure to shield the eyes and wrap the breaking object in a cloth to protect your hands—some lessons are learned the hard way. If it is a modern insulated window the breaking object needed might be something substantial, like a shovel. Which, of course, may be in the locked shed in the backyard, requiring yet another key.

NOTE: Your estate can be sued for damages, a higher level of curse than most folks imagine, so ease of corporeal recovery is a pretty big deal.

People have different habits around keys. Some people give up using them, figuring it is an illusion of security and an annoyance. Others load up like Fort Knox with padlocks, nailed windows, and keypads requiring codes, usually forgotten. Whatever your home security and accessibility is, think about what an EMT might have to do to enter your home, instead of imagining a criminal intent on stealing the flat-screen TV from the living room wall.

House keys are not the only keys necessary. Your car keys also need to be readily available as car relocation may be required. Most homes have a place for keys that is obvious, convenient for family and thieves alike. If your keys are labeled and together in one place, you earn points in the eyes of your heirs and other random people who want your stuff.

If you have keys in a drawer that don't seem to go to anything, the car is inaccessible, and the front door can't be locked with guaranteed reentry, your clean-up crew already hates you, at least a little.

Alarms are another issue. Sometimes they are cosmetic, left over from the previous owner, and only serve as a crime deterrent by appearance. Sometimes they make a terrifying racket but do nothing to alert actual emergency personnel. Unless someone knows the code to disarm, the alarm will continue until someone rips the alarm out of the wall, and even then, it might not stop wailing. It is amazing what folks will do to get an alarm to stop sounding—I have seen it firsthand—it is not pretty and the sound of the destruction echoes in your head as painfully as the alarm. If there is an alarm, the codes are more important than keys. All advice regarding sharing of keys also pertains to sharing alarm codes and instructions.

When you decide on trusted key and code holders, entrust them with these valuables with a ceremony using props to reinforce the importance of the event. Whiskey and blood oaths might work, but tailor the moment to the recipient and reinforce the responsibility by making them practice. If you stick an unlabeled key wrapped in a napkin with the alarm code scribbled in pencil in someone's purse, be aware you are cursing your clean-up crew.

The most useful aspect of alarms that notify emergency personnel is that when the alarm blasts, and it cannot be disarmed, eventually someone official appears. Don't be surprised if they have guns drawn and ask you to "exit the house with your Hands Up!" It is helpful if your people are crying and have their identification handy. This is not entirely a bad thing because officials need to be notified of your deceased state anyway. The blaring alarm saved your crew the effort of having to think of notifying the authorities.

Before moving on to what comes next, know that you have choices to make. You could buy a bunch of random keys, if you don't have them already, color code them as if they are important and dump them in a conspicuous drawer. You could never give anyone a backup key, change your access codes every week, and install an alarm system that screams and starts to smoke when activated. If you are leaning towards cursing your heirs, this is a prime opportunity. Be sure to install reinforced doors that require expensive tools to breach! Ghost or Guardian? Your choice.

THE BODY

The anticipation of finding someone's body that was last seen breathing, laughing, farting, and spilling tea is daunting. But unless there is a surprising mess involved, dead bodies are usually little trouble. And even if they are messy, there are experienced professionals qualified to handle them. You can help your team deal with your dead body by having a few reassuring conversations while alive. Tell them once dead, you won't care, and you won't complain anyway. And if you have concerns about the appearance of your cooling corpse, like one last shave, or a manicure, those things are better accomplished once you have been dead more than a few minutes and with the help of a mortuary (see chapter on Undertakers).

While traditions vary, at least initially, the only touching of the corpse is to take a pulse. No one should try to scoop you off the floor or pry you out of the recliner. If someone tries, all that happens is that officials yell at the person who tried to move the body. And the eager team member might have to visit the emergency room themselves for their newly injured back.

That warning aside, if you may not be completely and positively dead and CPR seems appropriate, all living humans should make the attempt to save you—even if their back is at risk! I encourage all readers to learn CPR, even if you are small and frail; this is an important skill for all alive humans. To spread the word, send your clean-up crew an email with links to a course, or show off your newly earned certificate of competence on Facebook or the fridge.

I was taught to time chest compressions to the refrain of the Queen song (1980), "Another one bites the dust." I suspect my instructor had a previous curse-like experience when dealing with the recently dead or their companions that led him to this snarky suggestion.

Also, no one should try to pull the family ring off your finger before you are packaged up by professionals. There is plenty of time for your heirs to squabble over your belongings, but this initial moment is not that time. If anyone is worried that jewels may go missing, even though they are likely fake—that surprise comes later—the cleanup crew should take a picture to prove the jewels were with you before you were ushered into the antiseptic world of the newly dead.

If you want to help, when you get an opportunity, you can kindly reassure your people that professionals are welcome to your remains. Emergency squad folk and the police are your family's best friends during this time. They have equipment to extricate you from the attic, where you expired swatting bats, or from the recliner that gobbled you up while watching your favorite show. All your cleanup team needs to do is turn off the TV, put out any open flame, take the cat to a temporary home, and lock the house. Then take care of themselves.

And no loved ones should return to clean your final resting place. No matter how neatly you accomplished your exit, people who delay doing their own laundry or seldom clean the toilets will not remember you fondly as they scrub your point of demise. The cleaning products under the sink are insufficient for cleaning up after dead bodies anyway. There are special companies that do this sort of thing and can deal with significant departure messes. It is less likely that you will make such a dramatic exit unless there is major drama in your life, and in that case the authorities might already be involved. If you are a recluse or an old meanie, it is unlikely you purchased this book, but if so—skip to the end of every chapter for advice on leaving your heirs special curses just for them.

If you died in a hospital or care facility, the professionals there are experienced in handling the recently dead. Eventually your family gets access to your body in a clean and sanitized environment. Retirement homes, assisted living centers, and hospices, all have resources that are comforting and should be investigated well before they are needed.

Many folks prefer to stay in their own familiar home and don't like all the meddling and rules that accompany professional assisted living accommodations. If you can pass for sound mind, and your purchase of this book is proof, and are able to follow the example of your children and go your own way without listening to advice or counsel, you may be living almost anywhere. You may live in a luxury condo your children covet, a yurt with goats your children do not covet, or more likely, a comfy dwelling that needs some tender loving care that you haven't gotten around to handling. The processing of newly dead people is different if you live in an adult facility of any kind compared to independent living situations where there are no routines in place for newly required body work. If you live by yourself this chapter on your Body is particularly important because amateurs may be first in the house when your farewell takes place. Just because you may go a bit cold before all the activity surrounding your demise gets started does not mean that was not exactly the leave taking you planned. You can expire by yourself and remain unattended for some time in the fanciest assisted living facility or nursing home. When it comes to your DDay, living on your own really just means there is no professional staff member at a desk in the lobby for your crew to call.

This can be a particularly fraught topic for families, and the elderly and infirm are often moved into group living situations that can be unsuitable but appear to be the only responsible option. Group living accommodations can be wonderful sociable places for folks. They can offer valuable companionship and necessary care, relief from home maintenance and innumerable conveniences. Just saying, the speed of finding a corpse is no reason to choose one.

If torture for survivors is in order, consider leaving a letter stating your fervent desire for exactly the opposite type of dwelling you inhabited on your DDay and lay a final guilt trip on those doing your ultimate dirty work.

REMAINING LIVING THINGS

When your body separates from your spirit and your pets, it is time to attend to the ultimate away from home planning.

Pets

Pets are often the most reliable and comforting companions for the elderly and infirm. Stories abound of magical dogs who called 911 by barking in dial tones, and cats who retrieved insulin and administered it through their own claws. Older folks sometimes stop keeping pets, not wanting to think about their animals outliving them and being unappreciated by the same people who may be neglecting them now.

Adult children sometimes have strong opinions about their parents' animal friends, conveniently forgetting the ferrets, fish, and iguanas they abandoned to their parents' care when they were young or traveled the world finding themselves.

I encourage anyone who sees death lurking, to indulge in animal companionship, up to the point where genuine neglect or abuse is likely. Forgetting to feed large animals can lead to your children skipping the chapters of this book referencing your bodily remains. Living with more vermin than necessary does nothing good for your pet or your psoriasis.

If you need help caring for your pet, ask for it, accept it if it is offered, and pay for it if you can, but do not jump first to the conclusion that your only constant companion be a battery-operated purring fur ball. Pet care services are used constantly by the not-even-close-to-dead people, so they can easily be arranged for the getting-closer-to-dead people.

A common situation is the loyal pet, guarding, washing, or sleeping next to your remains. Your clean-up crew must separate you from your companion and find appropriate placement for the grieving pet, while grieving and distraught themselves.

Encouragement of friendly relations among all pets and people concerned while everyone is breathing, is good preparation. Don't assume this makes the pet issue an easy one, although it is likely to help.

My mother adopted an abandoned white kitten when she was elderly. Found at a gas station and smudged with grease, it was adorably pitiful. I had complete confidence in my mother's ability to civilize this kitten as she had done for scores of animals before. In retrospect this was one of the earliest signs of my mother's failing capacities. Pay attention.

At first, I only noticed the occasional scratches on Mother's fragile skin. Then I realized the cat was hostile to visitors, but I didn't see it misbehave with my mother. When my mother died, I assumed naively that more active attention from a family member in good health would bring the cat to a more acceptable state of behavior. I placed the cat, Casper, with my extremely capable son who has always had a soft touch with animals and a spotless record of responsibility in this area.

At first the problems were about Casper playing in the window blinds and disturbing my son's sleep. The habit of biting when petted didn't seem insurmountable. True, Casper was alone much of the time, but cats sleep eighteen hours a day and are well known for their ability to entertain themselves.

My son arrived home one day and was flagged down by the parking lot attendant at his building. Turns out the police were called to his apartment because of loud music coming from his place while he was at work. Twice.

Casper learned how to turn on the music system, and then turn the dial to increase the volume. The police unplugged the system after their second visit, never having seen the cat in the apartment. Haunted condo? Absolutely.

I relieved my son of Casper duty and brought him home temporarily to my own menagerie. My zoo was already full, and I had the new responsibilities of my recently deceased mother to handle. I was invited to a cookout at a friend's home where miraculously I met a couple with a huge weakness for white cats. They had one that sat in the gentleman's lap through prolonged cancer treatment and had recently died. The cat, not the man.

I mentioned I needed to re-home my mother's white cat but that he was challenging and recounted his recent brushes with law enforcement. This sentimental, grieving couple begged to adopt Casper. Of course, I gratefully agreed but I kept in touch with them as I suspected this would be a temporary placement.

At first, I heard via my friend but not from

the adopters, that there were adjustment problems. Casper sometimes scratched and bit them, and occasionally indulged in surprise attacks. I inquired but they told me they adopted him for life, and I need not worry. It turned out that their subsequent adoption of a full-grown Husky sent Casper instantly into domesticity and the family to peace among the animals.

Casper was a special case, but there are as many varieties of pets as there are people, so special cases are the rule rather than the exception. You do your family an enormous service by considering the condition and temperament of your pets before anyone needs police backup or tranquilizer darts.

Consider every option, except depriving yourself of a wonderful companion. Who else will cuddle close while you have tea or a nice glass of wine in the late afternoon? Who else will wash your toes until they shine? Deprivation is not a solution of any kind but consider all other alternatives.

If you have already decided who is to take over the care of your pet(s), have them step in now when you are away or unable. Pay them for the service, and if they won't take your money, put it in a jar with their name on it. If you live with a pet no one else in your circle wants, let everyone know you are giving it the best years of its life, and do not insist on adoption by someone you know. There are placement services available for all sorts of pets and the most appropriate adoption is the most successful. That fit may not be found within your circle of people.

Curses in this case may result in animal abuse, so get busy and plan like a Guardian when it comes to pets.

Plants
As an example of another living thing that requires thoughtful planning, consider my giant staghorn fern. This fern was harvested from the rainforests of Puerto Rico in the 1950's by my father.

He managed to keep the fern growing and

thriving for 45 years in various suburban dwellings in Alabama, Virginia, and New Jersey with artificial light and watering systems. My father died in 1999 and the fern stayed with my mother until she died a few years later.

In 2024 it is six feet wide by six feet tall and six feet deep and required special consideration and a U-Haul when my husband and I moved from our farm to a more traditionally sized home. A place that met the needs of this fern was a required parameter in our home shopping. The realtor was confused by our need for a sunny indoor area that was too small for any normal human use but perfect for an enormous tropical plant.

I hope this fern doesn't end up in a dumpster, and I freely admit to caring more about the future of the living fern than I do about my own expired remains. I anticipate my eventual future in much less impressive condition although I am pondering options that may be esthetically pleasing.

The fern, however, still has potential to live on in glory. I have cultivated a relationship with a local botanical garden and this fern shall be the premier specimen of its kind in their collection. At least that's what I plan for. Nothing is certain, and I don't intend to haunt the living for fern neglect, but I made arrangements for this plant and hope this relieves my loved ones from feeling the need to build an addition on their homes for the giant fern. That is a curse.

Stowaways

Having covered pets and plants, you may fairly wonder what other living things bear consideration? I am not referring to anything that needs to be adopted or cared for, but things that can and should be exterminated or removed no matter how eco-friendly you and your friends may be.

Racoons under the porch, rats and bats in the eaves, mice in the cellar, fleas, flies, silverfish, bed bugs, and all other wiggly, squirmy things that may have taken up residence with you, invited and tolerated knowingly or not, need to make their exit before you do. Depending on the critter and the infestation, it may be time to take a small vacation while professionals deal with these problems before your loved ones must do it. Unless you really want your clean-up crew to hate you.

Stock certificates chewed by silverfish, and belongings that were cherished but infested, are guaranteed to gross out those you leave behind and diminish any value. As our health and cleanliness have improved, our tolerance for vermin has declined.

I have a friend who works with a small-town charitable group that evaluates local needs and raises money for small individual gifts. Someone may need a new refrigerator, or a window air conditioner and that relatively small thing can make a big difference in comfort and health. She visited an older lady who needed help with air conditioning and lawn care. While perched on the edge of an upholstered chair the charitable evaluator began to worry that a migraine was lurking. The worn carpeted floor seemed to be moving, sort of like one might imagine a gently waving magic carpet. The good news was that a headache was not arriving. The bad news was that the carpet was actually moving. It was undulating with the motion of stowaways living under the surface. No new vacuum could touch the challenge, but a qualified exterminator would help a lot.

Who knows? If you deal with stowaways now, whether you can see, hear, smell them or not, your personal condition may improve enough that you make it to the end of this book. Curse averted.

UNDERTAKERS

It is usually not difficult to find reputable mortuaries, and your best source of recommendations are friends and family with experience. Funeral service is a licensed profession in most states and so there are state regulations, professional associations and licensing boards. If you must stretch to find services nearby, or you live way too close to the locale of the recent headline featuring an unprofessional undertaker, this still should be a relatively easy task to check off your list.

I used two different funeral homes for four different deceased and found both to be extraordinarily helpful. Believe it or not, Yelp and other social media rate such services, but I found mine talking to friends at the local Lions Club and from a hospice caregiver's recommendation.

There are very good reasons we have mortuaries. Professionals there have experience with aspects of life that most of us do not have. And they have distance. Ideally, they are empathetic, kind, helpful and efficient, but best of all they are not busy weeping, cursing, or doing the leftover errands of the deceased. Yes, they can sell the grieving a casket that requires a mortgage, and yes, they may give Nana the face lift she never wanted, but they can also keep your body safely in storage while your family figures out what to do with you. They can clean you up and dress you in your favorite outfit, even if it hasn't fit in years. Your crew should enlist professionals to transfer your body from the place of your passing to the mortuary.

So now you are in temperature-controlled storage and depending on your cultural and religious traditions, the next steps take place swiftly, or at the leisure of the living.

I was once in a small European farm town for the wedding of a friend when an elderly family member unexpectedly died. With no mortuary in town, the deceased was stored in the walk-in refrigerator at the local Fest Hall. The tradition there was not to embalm, so refrigeration was important, as the burial was to take place after the completion of the wedding ceremony and celebration.

It was especially convenient that the same folks who were attending the wedding would be attending the funeral. As visitors kept arriving for the wedding, there were frequent visits to Aunt Monika in the fridge.

In this case fewer visitors might have been better, but she was buried just in time and before significant transformations and decay began to occur. My mother was with me, and despite not knowing the language, she was crystal clear on the need for swift action after the wedding given the expressions and conversational tones of visitors to the dear departed.

Expect small European farm towns to be matter of fact about these matters. Blunt as they are, their local cemeteries are beautiful, with each grave adorned with living flowers and tended by their families. Having spent many hours "visiting the dead people" with my son, I am reconsidering having a plot somewhere even if ashes alone will be interred, or maybe there could be a plaque in a garden. Like you, I need to do something about it.

Despite their near universal helpfulness, steel yourself to meet with the mortician. They present options to you that you never imagined and have likely had requests made of them that could fill another book. The one that stunned me was the option to have the fingerprints of my loved one etched on a gold pendant or onto a clear paperweight. Save your clean-up crew from these considerations by reviewing them yourself and indicating your wishes and instructions.

Mortuary marketing is not light reading and you had better do it away from the mortuary because I encourage laughter and you may sense the dead who have made different choices won't appreciate your snickering. For true guardianship status, designate, coordinate, and purchase your mortuary services and accoutrements prior to your passing.

Funeral homes also know things that you don't know and give you checklists you need to consider. Guess what? Social Security already knows you are dead if you die in any facility with official records. They stop paying you immediately!

Mortuaries routinely help with car donations and transportation needs of various kinds. Not all funeral homes handle cremation, but most do, so make that assumption and don't spend extra time searching around for a cremation-only business unless you have specific needs or live somewhere you know that is a rarity.

Ask about whatever concerns you the most and it is likely the undertaker has undertaken a concern like yours before. They always ask if there is a Will because that is a document that may have instructions for them. The reason you are spending time visiting Funeral homes is that you are the model of good scout preparedness, and feel free to tell them what is or is not their business.

Despite the dramatic pushiness of undertakers on television, this does not reflect my experience. And if the undertaker is talking with a living person who is not grieving for someone but is considering their own needs, the dynamic of the meeting is changed and tendencies toward up-selling are less likely or effective.

The mortuary often handles the ordering of Death Certificates too, which is essential for your heirs to have in order to complete any work on your estate. Certified copies of your Death Certificate are required for many things and your clean-up crew will need several copies.

Official Certified Copies are required for most

financial and legal entities, so if you have twenty-four bank accounts to protect you in case local banks went under, one Certified Death Certificate is needed for each of these accounts.

In many cases the official Death Certificate is returned once the bank/insurance company/tax office is finished with it. If your heirs want to tackle one job at a time while waiting weeks or months for its return, fewer copies may be needed. If they want to tackle as many jobs at one time as possible, they should order more Death Certificates. Time no longer matters to you but if time matters to your clean-up crew it is easier and faster to get a few too many Death Certificates now than to face delays ordering more later.

I have used various synonyms for the same profession throughout this chapter and they all have different historical roots but refer to the same service. You are unlikely to only need the services of a grave digger or a friend with a backhoe unless you live remotely, in which case please have your family contact me and tell me which sections of this book require circumstantial addenda. This is a pretty easy set of tasks because qualified strangers do the dirty work.

You can barely plan an effective post-life curse because professionals are involved. The worst case is if your heirs have different opinions as to which mortuary merits the storage of what remains of you. It is best for you to go ahead and pay for what you want in advance. Of all the things that speak to the living from beyond, money has a particularly loud voice.

YOUR CORPSE
(Let the Fighting Begin)

Once you are safely in the fridge at the mortuary awaiting what comes next you can still help your family with your dead body, and they need help. The ideal time for prep work is while you are still breathing, and able to yell, whisper, tease and cajole. If you leave behind one or two committed souls who follow your prescribed wishes exactly, all you need to do is make those wishes clear in writing and pay for them. If you leave behind a raucous crew who cannot agree on where to go to dinner, this is the beginning of a serious test of your reach beyond your living years.

You can warm up your people by lightly mentioning your demise at every opportunity. Or by threatening everyone sternly if that is your style. This is a creative opportunity, and discussions may prompt new solutions not yet imagined.

If you are not planning a post-life curse, then you can make a habit of adding that there are no bonus rewards for wishes carried out exactly, so no big deal. You will be past assigning retribution. Unless you proceed to make elaborate plans to punish failure of post life wish fulfillment. If cursing is your plan, this is your opportunity to live your dream after your death.

Sneaking onto the university football field, singing the fight song and spreading your ashes requires a lot of "tuning up" in advance and your dedicated team may be at risk of jail time. The

Kilauea Volcano plan where your ashes and whiskey are committed to the fiery depths requires substantial capital and your team probably doesn't have your money yet.

My husband spoke rapturously of being set alight in a flaming boat à la Vikings of yore, until he started hearing talk among our friends planning for the event. It sounded like so much fun for the living that he began to wonder if we would wait for him to die before getting the party started.

He was already building a wooden kayak and was planning to dredge a pond on the farm before getting nervous about how much he was encouraging us. The pond was eventually completed, but the kayak is still unfinished. He couldn't resist putting it in the pond to be sure it floats but the final touches remain to be done and I suspect will remain so, to prevent premature cast off.

Personally, I lean toward a back-to-nature theme. My ashes can be mixed into a glaze to paint a ceramic pot. I even found an artist with experience, although only with the ashes of a German Shepherd. And when the pot breaks, my glaze-ashes can then assist in the drainage at the roots of some cool plant or huge fern. Or a ceramic dish in a garden? I need to decide.

There are details of every sort you might consider. What about your hairdo or your clothing? Is there special music you want to play or a choir you want to sing? What about a wake, and do you have plans for what everyone should drink?

I read of a tribe that carves elaborate coffins that particularly suit the deceased. I drive a lot and it might be fitting to lower me into the earth in my big blue truck with stiff me posed waving out the window.

The Dogon plateau people in Mali perform ritual funeral dances for those who have died in the past year or so with elaborate ritual masks. A funeral dance might be fun, but I would have to leave instructions for my band preferences listed in order, in case they break up or aren't available.

Do you want a traditional service at a place

of worship and a luncheon after, followed by the rowdy party where everyone weighs in on the wisdom, creativity or pain in the butt you and your last wishes were? Will half of the family boycott your funeral if they have left for a new church across the county?

If you have strong feelings about where, and in what manner your remains should rest, you must write them down and you must pay for them in advance. Leave a post-it on this page telling your family where to look for the receipt or the jar of cash. It bears repeating—there is less arguing if the bill has been paid.

And just because you did not buy a plot and leave instructions for your grave marker appearance, text, coffin specs, and service details does not mean you can't torture people with complex ash scattering plans. You can pay extra and have the mortician package your ashes into as many containers as you like, and that is way better than spilling your dustiness out on the kitchen table for division into Ziploc bags.

There are rules about the transport of human remains in checked baggage that should be considered in these days of TSA inspection of unidentified powders. Mortuaries ask if remains are to be dealt with locally or transported and they can provide instructions and packing supplies.

When transporting my brother's remains, I presented my luggage with the official forms at the airline baggage check. It was obvious that I was the only one around who knew the rules. The officials put a lot of extra tape around my suitcase containing a box of human remains, quickly glanced at the paperwork, and scooted away from my bag wishing me safe travels. Better some creeped-out employees than my brother dumped out for extra TSA inspection, a fate he would have resented. I did not risk his haunting me.

Mailing human remains is also possible and may save complicated personal transport across state lines. State police are not convinced of the need for speed by the distracted and bereaved, and your crew can simply ship you to your final destination. When someone walks into a post office with the well-marked Human Remains carton, they get to the front of the line in no time.

The biggest challenge is if your family fights over your corpse and you have cursed them all by not providing any guidance. Careful consideration of your last wishes is vital. Be sure if you are going to torture the living, do it on purpose.

INSTRUCTIONS AND MESSAGES FROM BEYOND

Whatever you decide, post death instructions must be available to your heirs. It is imperative that more than one person you leave behind knows where messages from you can be found. And if there are very few or no people you leave behind and your demise is left to police, EMTs, lawyers, bankers and government officials you do not know, your last wishes must be obvious and clear. If they are not, in the name of convenience for the living and unconcerned, nothing proceeds according to your wishes unless by chance, and everything is decided by the state and unknown strangers. People need to know where to look without consulting a psychic or digging through composting paper under your desk.

If you have no wishes or concerns about what happens after you die, the question is, "Does anyone else?" If there are those who do, then would you like to help them? Or "Phooey! Curses on them all!"

Messages about your body
DNR

No matter how well you feel, the day you are about to conclude your non-emergency medical visit and are handed a neon-colored form with the words in bold letters indicating DNR, consider this a sign that you better motor through this book quickly.

In this case DNR does not stand for Department of Natural Resources and no one is offering you a Senior discount on a hunting license. This DNR stands for Do Not Resuscitate and provides instructions to post the neon form in plain sight in your home, preferably in a high traffic area. Historically this might have been by a landline, but now it might just be plastered on the refrigerator. The idea is that if EMT folks are running to your aid they can quickly see how much aid you want provided.

When I first encountered the dreaded DNR form I was thankfully not personally being talked to in a loud, slow speaking voice in the persistent habit of health professionals who assume everyone older than they are is deaf. I was accompanying my sister-in-law to a routine medical checkup.

She made the appointment herself and walked in without assistance, but she was extremely thin and deep into her eighties. The doctor had directed her to eat more and gain weight, a message he had repeated for at least twenty years. In the forty years I had known her, she was always thin. He also berated her for her persistent Cognac habit, even though her lab tests indicated all her organs were functioning normally. If she hadn't been honest with the doctor about this habit, he wouldn't have known about the Cognac. Very fine Cognac.

As we checked out, I was handed a bright yellow form and was told that I (not we) should look it over. I (we) ignored it until we got home after a nice lunch including a couple of glasses of wine. Before I left, I remembered to look through the pile of papers from the doctor's office. The neon one jumped out, as it was meant to do, and I sat down next to my sister-in-law and suggested it might be time to have some Cognac.

There were typical questions about her preferences regarding resuscitation and CPR. We talked about them while I internally considered that everyone should give these questions some thought. Not so different from the Living Will questions that we tend to neglect until we can barely speak, what medical treatments do you want or oppose, and what about pain management or organ donation?

It is doubtful you can be treated in any medical facility today without being asked about the status of your Living Will, but unless you are on death's door, no one presses the issue. Once this info is posted on your fridge in Day-Glo colors, which you can't avoid seeing whenever you want a glass of milk, you may be startled into action. Am I so close to death that we need neon? Maybe I should buy one apple at a time?

Turns out there are more ways to post this information and with a little imagination you might have some fun with it. Have you always wanted a tattoo? Guess what? Your last wishes regarding your resuscitation can be colorfully inked on your boobs! Good idea to have the tattoo on the front of your body since they may not flip you over until they have accidentally saved you when you may have been opposed to that choice.

If you were a volunteer subject for Ink Masters and no one can sort out the instructional tattoos from the ones you got when you were drunk, this option is less useful. And what if you change your mind? Complicated. Or jewelry? The Medic Alert bracelets are not very stylish but you can make an artistic and fashionable choice. What if you have your wishes engraved on a fine piece of jewelry with gemstones so large that no one can ignore it? Wonder which one of your heirs wants to grab that for their very own?

LIVING WILL

I mentioned a Living Will in passing, partly because you cannot step near a medical facility without someone asking you if you have one, and if so, is it in your file? If you don't have one and want one, they give one to you for free. Most of us have several with contradictory instructions on file all over the place.

Complete a Living Will, date it and sign it, and hang it by the vivid DNR form and you are covered and done. Laws vary on the legality of these across states and countries so consult the all-knowing internet or someone at your local healthcare facility.

A potential unanticipated benefit of the new flashy notices about your death wishes on the fridge is that they stimulate discussion with loved ones. Now that you are working through this guidebook, you have some structure for addressing these critical issues with friends and family. If the people who you want to share this information with are adults and sane, the time for sharing may as well be now.

If your loved ones are children, stick the forms above their eyesight on the fridge and consider your work finished. Planning is something to praise rather than disparage and you are showing off your fitness to continue living as you wish with consideration for those you leave behind. If you are too lively to need these forms in plain sight, it still is time to share your wishes and the location of important documents with other consenting adults. They are not interested in having this discussion and are afraid to think about the topic but tell them anyway and then drop it. They will not forget. I promise—you got their attention.

Fireproof safes

Fireproof safes are a solid home investment and are great holiday gifts. It is an even better gift if the Gifter installs the safe where the Giftee would like it to stay for the rest of their life. And if you only need a fireproof safe the size of a shoebox, don't accept a free one the size of the coffin you may be trying on soon. Those suckers are heavy. When my father told me the location of theirs, I freaked out a little. I was in denial that my parents were closer to their last days than I wanted to admit. On some level though, I was glad I knew where it was.

They didn't have a large house, but I was not thinking clearly when they died. I would have been more distraught without the information I needed to do whatever it was that I was about to discover I needed to do!

Give some thought to the location of the home safe. Most of us go to extremes to make it difficult for thieves to find, but they only want your easily fenced valuables and your digital identity and not the fireproof safe in the closet you haven't had the courage to open in years.

Also consider if it might cause you more embarrassment than you would like at the end of the day. The box of porn next to the safe will be the topic of family whisperings for years. "Are those photos of someone we know?"

If nothing in your house is tidy, make this the one neat spot. It should also be a place where idle children won't wander and make paper airplanes out of the receipt from the cemetery. And the safe should be closed and latched. It does not have to be locked, but if that 'fireproof' concept is to have any meaning at all, it must be closed.

Firearms of any kind, loaded or not, should be far from your safe of controversial instructions and official documents. Old love letters and photos of the girl you never told your wife about are dealt with in another chapter.

Safe deposit boxes and banks
These are useful but less popular than they once

were with the advent of home fireproof safes and the decline of neighborhood banks. If you have one, keep a key for yourself and give one to your responsible heir of choice that promises to be helpful, especially if that heir is a co-signer on your bank account.

It was mentioned at the beginning under "KEYS," but again, get rid of old keys to unused storage lockers, abandoned safe deposit boxes, and lovers' homes. These are confusing, potentially upsetting, or lead to bogus treasure hunts that disappoint your survivors. And be sure your bank hasn't changed names or gone out of business.

My brother was disappointed in a bank investment he made. He was so disappointed that he stopped opening all mail from the bank and left it stacked in a tall, dusty pile which was infested with silverfish by the time I got to it.

He did not respond to any instructive mail for over seven years. During these years there were mergers, buyouts, and calls for stock options.

When I met this sad pile, it was a challenge to navigate but I was determined. I was pretty sure there wasn't a pot of gold at the end of the dusty rainbow, but I was determined to do my best and be responsible. Eventually I discovered that the bank assets had been purchased by a private company and there was no public stock traded. If I knew the exact value of the stock, then I could claim the asset from the bank as his heir. But I couldn't know the value of the stock unless the bank told me what it was.

Surprisingly, this is not an uncommon situation where you must know a fact before you are allowed to learn the exact same fact. And while I was wading through this mess, eager private companies who found the account on unclaimed property lists were happy to attempt to claim it for me for a fee. Those lists are public records and can be found by searching through state government websites—in your spare time.

I decided that I did not want to deal with the company that claimed it could get my brother's funds for a percentage of the value, as a point of principle. And exhaustion. I don't know if they could have done what they said they could do or not, and I was pretty sure I was not forfeiting much money. I would definitely forfeit my time and energy which was waning. If a company like this charges you nothing other than their commission if they succeed, and the disclosures they require don't alarm you, it may be worth a try.

All states keep websites where you can search for unclaimed property in your name or a decedent's name. These state sites are the best places to start if you think there are some valuables worth pursuing. After a defined period, the assets revert to the state monitoring them and you have made a donation without getting to claim a tax deduction. Generosity personified.

The issue for a bank which may try to help you claim such funds has to do with a requirement that they guarantee the transaction. If they don't know the exact value in advance, they are opening themselves up to fraud and guaranteeing payment of an unknown amount. It is the kind of conundrum that leads your heirs to curse you. The dust and silverfish don't help either.

Tracking down unclaimed assets, and unclaimable assets, is guaranteed to make your family mad. No telling what they will engrave on your tomb if you tick them off now. And the annoyance may continue for years. I recently received a letter instructing my deceased sister-in-law, four years passed, how she, now me, could claim an insurance underpayment of $10. Tempting.

Contents of Safe—Documentation—Checklist
This is not an all-inclusive list, but if you have most of these documents, anything missing should be available to your heirs from this starting point. Your clean-up crew should be made aware that regardless of their preparedness when someone walks into the bank of the deceased, the Post Office to change an address, or the newly empty home, they should expect to meet an official asking for a document they have never seen or heard

of. The attitude to take is exhausted, bereaved desperation, which is easy because it's probably true.

The folks interrogating your clean-up crew are tired too and your representatives are preventing these underappreciated officials from getting back to their own bills, jobs, and families. And they have either been in the same situation or anticipate that they will find themselves in those sorry shoes before long. Everyone needs to ask for help; be as nice and pathetic as possible, and try to find the documents listed below. Funeral directors often offer a list like this one, as will insurance companies. Cross check any lists you are given and do what is applicable.

If you can organize all this right now while you are breathing, you are one fantastic Guardian.

Document Checklist

- Birth certificate
- Death Certificates (multiple copies)—once you are dead
- Marriage licenses—government issued, not just from a church
- Last Will and Testament
- Power of Attorney
- Medical Power of Attorney (unless the body is cold)
- Military discharge papers
- Funeral instructions and receipts
- Mortgages and deeds
- Financial records
- Tax returns—if you were living any part of a calendar year and there was income, a return must be filed.
- Stock certificates
- Bank records
- Insurance and annuities
- Trust documents

This book on your desk

You have dropped hints about what you want to happen to your body when you die like a kid hinting for a birthday present. You have a safe place where instructions and receipts for prepayment into your place of rest can be found and the place is not embarrassing to you or your heirs and they know where it is.

So far so good, unless you really don't know what you would like to happen when you are dead and are past pondering the options. In that case having all this organized documentation validates for all those who loved you, or pretended to love you, that you could never make up your mind.

Be a sport and go ahead with Plan A even if you are not sure you prefer it to Plan B or C. Flip a coin. Make up sealed envelopes, mix them up, and pull one out of a hat and discard the losers. Don't even peek! Do your family a favor by being the pain in the ass for all you left behind. You are dead after all. Do your share! Death is no excuse.

In fact, you are likely to become the new favorite scapegoat.

We all have been grateful to have a pet in the room when a nasty smell emanated from our nether regions. When an important document is mislaid, the dog must have eaten it. My cats have peed on everything from the contents of my mother-in-law's suitcase to my favorite shearling slippers.

As the most recently dead member of the family, you can now lighten the load for everyone else by shouldering the burden of your last wishes. They can blame you, they can toast you, or they can ignore you, but by being clear about your desires they don't get to play the game of, "That's what I know she would have wanted."

Your goal in reading this book and working through it is to take that game off the table and encourage drinking games like flip cup or craps. Leave this book highlighted on your desk so they know how far you made it before DDay. They need to deal with you and your mess, and they don't want to do it. Do some light housekeeping now and be a Guardian hero.

OBITUARY—MEMORIAL— AFTER-PARTY CHECKLIST

The Obituary and the Memorial are interconnected, as one doesn't easily occur without the other. And they are ASAP items if either is going to happen close in time to your departure.

If there is to be a memorial service, rye-filled wake, or quiet acceptance of visitors, people need to know that you are dead. You have cooked up scores of guest lists in your lifetime and the point has always been to invite who you must and try to include those you really want at the party. This is not much different. There are notices in newspapers where you have lived, and family and friends must be called, and this is not a job for email unless that is your only means of contact.

If social media is your thing and more importantly, the favorite means of communication by your loved ones, that offers another opportunity for clear communication about plans. Ideally all plans can be made and finalized before anyone not intimately involved wades in and makes suggestions.

Old war buddies may prefer getting news via smoke signals and happily arm themselves for your well-deserved 21-gun salute. While well meaning, your pacifist children don't need this kind of help and may be properly fearful that more funerals will follow in quick succession if there are weapons at yours.

A Christmas card list with phone numbers is a good thing to leave stuck in the pages of this book. Your crew is able to use this list as if they were canvassing for an election. If they know your friends, it may be easier depending on whether they liked them or not, but either way, a list like this or an updated address book, paper or electronic, carefully stored with this book, can be a source of unanticipated help for your family.

The designated caller should begin with the first letter of your last name and call everyone in that section. They should do this because it includes your relatives who then send out word to other relatives your children may not know exist. There have been years when my holiday greetings only went to those sharing the first letter of my last name. Starting at "A" has gotten me into really big trouble if I didn't get too far in the holiday card process, and slighted friends and family will be annoyed, if not worse, if they don't know you are dead until the card they send is returned, "No such person at this address."

What follows is the script for contact calls. Go ahead and leave the actual message on an answering machine to avoid endless call backs.

1. Personal introduction of the caller asking for the addressee 'My name is…'
2. Info of your demise and funeral arrangements (location, date, and time)
3. Phone number of person they might call if they have questions or potential helpful thoughts. It is your choice if this is a real person or fake number.

As you read this you can imagine who might be good at this chore. It is busy work, and many people appreciate having something to do to help avoid facing personal grief. Sometimes doing a task that is deliberately devoid of feeling is especially welcome. People fight for this job, so consider delegating in advance.

In some cases, this is the perfect assignment for a family friend who won't leave sobbing messages on answering machines. There is too much potential for confusion, unnecessary worry, and setting off a flurry of misunderstanding. The recipient of a sobbing unintelligible call may think someone dear to them is in trouble, when it is only you that is dead. You can also hire a stranger, preferably an actor, who can show some empathy.

The Obit
You have saved your loved ones a lot of trouble with instructions as to what newspapers to notify, whom to call and who will get the calling

done, and what to say in the notices, online or in print. The obit can be left to the living, or you can write it yourself. If it is left to the living you are creeping into the 'curse' territory. In these days of emailing, you are opening Pandora's box of editing, bickering, and secretly adding and subtracting parts before submission by those who assume they should have a say.

Occasionally there is good reason to leave the obit to the living if someone you leave behind may offer you some privilege you may or may not deserve by virtue of their standing in the community. I once read a laudatory full-page obituary in a local newspaper for a man who died under suspicious circumstances. It was written by his soon to be ex-wife, and it very well may have gotten him into the burial ground of his choice.

If you choose to write it yourself the content and style are entirely up to you. If you have a flair for creative writing you may as well let it fly. After all, most of those who might contradict you are dead too or may be blessed with well-known unreliable memory. If your family thinks it is a joke they may not go along with your plan, so use some judgement as to what stories you include. And you thought this wasn't going to be any fun!

There are journalistic templates available to guide you and yours in composing your obituary. Traditionally Obits are objective life summaries with surviving and pre-deceased family members listed and information for the public on your service and next earthly destination. Those guidelines are less the trend these days so feel free to write what feels appropriate and let editors worry about what they publish. At least at your After-Party the obit will be available exactly as you want.

My mother received an award near the end of her professional life at age seventy-six, and repeatedly mentioned to me that the info for the introduction she provided for that event would make a great obit. She was absolutely right, but I didn't find it until eight years after she died. Go ahead and slip your favorite phrase or write up about yourself in the back of this book, next to the prepaid cemetery receipt. My failure to find the intro my mom referenced haunted me for years. When I found it, I wanted to mail it to everyone who came to her service.

The funeral director asks for an obituary and a picture of you, to send out and post online. If you have strong feelings about what picture, if any, is included in your obituary, go ahead and pick that out for your clean-up crew too. Believe it or not, Funeral Homes sometimes sponsor funeral planning meetings at restaurants and Senior Portrait opportunities, which give that particular photo-shoot category a whole new meaning. And in the name of diminishing someone's unrealistic expectations, the New York Times will not print your obit because you were a veteran and lived to be one-hundred-and-two years old. There are a lot of dead people in New York City.

The Memorial/After Party
Memorial arrangements are referenced in your obit but the details of the event itself can be

pondered, fought over, planned, and replanned until the date of the event. Some traditions avoid excessive planning time by requiring your remains be dealt with quickly. It is possible to delay whatever service is contemplated and the management of your remains as long as the mortuary is willing to accommodate you.

If your remains are in a small box, unsurprisingly they are much more willing to accommodate than if you are in a very large box or no box at all. The small box prompts calls reassuring your family about your safety on the peaceful shelves among others also resting in silence. The large box prompts calls of a more urgent nature.

If your religion dictates certain protocols, then thank your God for saving you and yours some trouble. Even if many decisions are off the table there may still be issues of music selection, songs to be sung, readings, who reads, who speaks about you and what they say—appreciated and appropriate or not.

Flowers, programs, donation sites, photographic displays, receiving lines, and post funeral eating and drinking are all things that require decision making and information sharing. Funeral homes can prompt you, so you don't miss any considerations and most of their websites enable online action by those reading the news of your Earthly exit.

Removing any decisions from the hands of your family and friends is appreciated even if they hate your choices, because it is one less thing they must consider. Otherwise, competitive siblings find issues to dispute and count personal wins and losses in the printed program. Children may be expected to kiss embalmed bodies in one last goodbye. There will be crying. Sometimes loud sobbing. You may find the various aspects of the memorial consoling or revolting, but if you make some choices now you are heading toward Angelic status with eternal wind at your back.

Memorial Checklist

- Location
- Time
- Transportation
- Music
- Readings/speakers/ushers
- Reception style/decorations/Flowers
- Photos/video
- Tissues/umbrellas/parking
- Guest book
- Program
- Donation info/collection basket
- Receiving lines (standing support)
- Burial/ash scattering attendees
- Post service eating and drinking attendees and invitees
- Celebration of Life Re-Defined

All this party planning and anticipation of dear ones coming together without you may be leaving you feeling kind of blue. You don't have to miss the party. Really.

A friend of mine suffered a rather sudden and determined cancer in her fifties. She was a fun-loving soul and found she could face the cancer which had a plan completely in conflict with her own, but she did not want to miss her own party.

Her family and friends took her wishes seriously and threw her the Celebration of Life Party of her dreams. Everyone she wanted to see made the effort to get there and party with her in person one last time. The funeral a few weeks later was much less fun but made more so by everyone talking about the party of two weeks before.

A similar event occurs when Grandma is doing very poorly, and everyone is called to visit before it is too late. My husband's grandparents kept this style of reunion party going for almost twenty years, during which time the family gathered from all over the country on a more regular basis than was our custom. Clever grandparents.

They got us in the habit of gathering whether anyone was threatening to die or not. We continue doing it still. A Guardian move on their part.

Memorials and Celebrations of Life often provide moments of joy and laughter even as emotions run high and there is mascara smearing everywhere you turn. Most attendees will come in sincere dedication to your memory and to experience the unique society of friends and family you brought together in life. If you were funny and joyful or gloomy and pessimistic, the folks who attend your terminal event will reflect your life and there is no harm in enjoying what you can in the company of others who may not be together again since the glue of the occasion has departed.

I attended the Celebration of Life of the brother of a dear friend. Since I knew the family well, I knew what to expect: a sad but genuinely celebratory crowd, all happy to see each other, share stories, and gently laugh at the more eccentric and endearing habits of the departed while consoling one another in their loss.

I noticed some elderly gentlemen I had not previously met and was introduced to them throughout the afternoon with each of them explaining confidentiality, "I'm one of the ROMEOs." As a group they did not match any experience I had of a Romeo type and were all over eighty years old and in various physical states suggesting health-precluding romantic activity. Eventually I was able to ask my friend if she knew anything about all the ROMEOs in attendance? Was this a secret society, or throwback to wild youth?

Turns out the ROMEOs are a friendly group of Retired Old Men Eating Out. I should have asked for restaurant recommendations. Pretty sweet legacy. Guardian for sure.

MAIL, CALL FORWARDING, EMAIL, SOCIAL MEDIA

They got through the memorial service with only minor bickering and moderate hangovers. You have been feted in the way you wished if you took the time to put it in writing and with payments rendered. Your bodily remains no longer remain inconveniently sitting around like cold pizza on Sunday morning. Before we get to estate issues, if you leave anything behind more than fond memories and a digital footprint, there is the paper trail of life. The more work your heirs must do to clean up after you, the less they care about their loss. And why did you have to take your leave just now? %&*$^*!

Mail

No matter what, bills must be paid. Your heirs must collect your mail ASAP and fill out the USPS form to have your mail forwarded to a responsible, obsessive compulsive family member.

The personality trait of this designee is important otherwise, all your bills get lost on the kitchen table mixed with the bills of the newly bereaved. This complicates things rather than cleans up your mess. If you can specify in advance, who the winner of your life lottery of paperwork is, do it now. Without your help there are disagreements, recriminations and delays. If your mortgage and taxes are not paid there is nothing like foreclosure to upset those you leave behind.

The other trick about USPS mail forwarding is that the form requires a signature of the person whose mail is being forwarded. Do I have your attention?

It may be that you have wisely delegated postal and bill paying duties to someone while you were breathing so this is not a problem now that your breathing has ceased. That step so many adult children discuss with sadness, when Mom can no longer keep up with bills and mail, can be something you secretly celebrate during your life.

I hate opening mail. There is almost nothing that arrives in the mail that I enjoy. Most of it is a condensed stack of trees I would rather see standing. Once my husband insisted on waiting to leave for a vacation until the mail came. He does not pay the bills in our household. When the eagerly awaited mail arrived, it included a notice that we were being audited by the IRS. This was a rough start to a needed vacation.

My son has aggressively fought spam, junk,

and snail mail for years. He has his bills electronically transmitted (see following section on email) and has almost beaten down the unremitting surge of paper mail attacks. I say "almost" because the fight is never over. Someone sends you a gift from a company and that company captures your address or email and begins their campaign to capture you and your money through your mailboxes.

You know, this young man has all the fine qualities required to take over my bills and mail today! Why wait? Just how much dementia must I pretend to have, is the question. I don't want anyone to start eyeing my blue truck!

Call forwarding/phones

If you have a phone, people call. They may even call you to chat when you are dead, forgetting that you are deaf to such earthly sirens. There are negatives and attention must be paid, but it is better to leave your phones working for three months postmortem, than to shut them off immediately.

I am not addressing the wisdom of smartphones in the hands of people who are not as smart as they once were and still consider themselves to be. But sticking to whatever phones you have once you are past answering them, call forwarding is the answer for landlines and cell phones alike. Text messages also may need to be forwarded.

The family member at the receiving end of calls and texts forwarded needn't be as detail oriented as the mail task master. This person should be able to take a call without breaking down but can anticipate the end of the job coming soon if they handle the calls and texts regularly and without too much delay. Once callers and texters are notified of your passing the ringing usually stops pretty fast. Even spammers stop bugging the dead. What is hoped is that this task brings to a graceful close your phone messaging world.

On a more sentimental note, I have trouble erasing funny text and recorded messages from people dear to me, and I am not alone. Know that someone may save a message from you for the rest of their life. Remember that when you are summarily asked to "leave a message," you may speak for eons from the grave.

And if there is a cell phone, there are photos. Someone needs to step up and offer to organize, edit, and file the photos on your phone that you never organized, edited, or filed. It is possible that you can spread this largesse while putting the work off onto your crew by sharing the entire mess with significant others, but know that means the photos will disappear into some cloud that may eventually be corrupted and fall from the sky.

There are professionals who can help with photo archives and if your budget allows, a consultation to develop a plan of action is a great place to start. And get recommendations. Your life photo archive should not land in amateur hands any more than your wedding video.

Email and Social Media

The thing about email is that it does not stop. And despite the growing junk pile, it shouldn't stop for a good while. The issue is the access required. This is another area where passwords are handy. And there are many ways to keep your myriad passwords secure, but in the end, someone needs your passwords, and you want them to have them. Fingerprint access and facial recognition are gross ideas once you are dead.

I read an article about passwords in Wired Magazine, a pretty reliable source for personal computer kinds of things. The article was the only one in the issue that I understood, but it spoke clearly to me.

A professional computer expert had his computer accounts hacked and wiped out because a teenager wanted his username. The author tracked down the hacker and he confessed his motive.

No big deal in that no one was holding his info for ransom or stealing banking data, but there were no longer any accessible files in the Cloud, or on the Earth, that contained the photographs of his family and their lifetime together, and nothing could get them back. Don't assume there is a way just because there always is on TV.

The author concluded that two-step access would have prevented his heartbreaking loss and recommended that you should have all your passwords and two-step authenticator typed up neatly on paper and stored in a safe place. And we have already spoken about safe places.

Since that article was published many, many more have been published on the same thing. If we weren't all so hooked on the wonders of computer access to the world, we would likely melt them down, drive over them, and head to the woods. But here we are, going to die and leave active email and social media accounts that live on without us.

Make sure someone reliable can find your passwords to access this world. For one thing, you may have bills that are automatically paid from bank accounts that eventually dry up once you have been dead for a while. Different email servers and social media accounts have different rules about how to finally sign off and delete your accounts, and do not assume this task will be quick or easy. The main thing is unless someone can access those accounts, your digital life continues, and it is not the afterlife you hoped for. I feel a curse coming on.

How effective are you at monitoring your own social media accounts for hacking and abuse? Now assume you keep your deceased mother's Facebook account open because it reminds you of her, her friends, her life, and has all sorts of entertaining threads. It is possible that this scenario is a happy one indefinitely. It is also possible that someone hacks her account, sends all her contacts emails selling them computer software that infects their computers and opens them to terrifying vulnerability. Unmonitored social media accounts are an entertaining potential hazard, but a hazard just the same. Inadvertent curses are the worst.

Part Two
YOUR ESTATE

Now that you are out of the way, there is still a paper trail.

Now that you have left the building, tears have dried up and the friends and family that don't want any of your belongings have made their exit, all that remains is your stuff. If someone reading this has been following along and doing homework, the keys to your remaining kingdom are in their hands and they can move forward to neatly tie up your affairs.

If you were wealthy, your affairs may be complicated depending on how much preparation you did ahead of your DDay. If you were not wealthy, there may be less to clean up, but that does not mean people will not fight about what remains.

CASH

Soon after my father died and was buried Mom's life settled down. She could get around but was not exactly agile. She suggested that I look under the rug under Dad's desk. That physical act would likely have killed her if she tried it.

Turns out, unbeknownst to me and my brother, Dad always kept a stash of cash, just in case. In case of what, I can only imagine, but sure enough, under the rug beneath the desk was an envelope of cash. It is likely many dearly deceased have left this earth, leaving their secret stash to be thrown out with the trash or pocketed by the experienced death cleaning crew. More on them later. Plan for your cash stash now, while you can.

If you have a pile of money hidden somewhere it would be generous of you to tell some deserving soul where they can find it. It is up to your heirs to share the news with others per your instructions or their conscience. If the cash is needed to help with any of your final business, like burial expenses or dumpster rental, it is important that someone responsible knows about this asset, and much better if the directions to the treasure are written down and kept in a safe place.

When the sibling who hates birds happily walks out with your noisy parrot, it is unlikely the secret compartment filled with Benjamins underneath the newspaper covered in bird poop is dreamt of by anyone other than the recipient of your trust. If people start showing up to 'help' at your house with metal detectors and then start pacing the yard, soon the whole family is out there digging up everything.

If it is common knowledge that you hide cash on your property, this is a golden opportunity for haunting and torturing everyone who annoyed you while you lived. It only takes some off-hand remarks about possible hiding places to set off the scavenger hunt of a lifetime.

It is tempting since it is so easy, and if you need some entertainment, consider a family cash scavenger hunt. Be prepared for some damage to your garden, so make sure they are digging around where you might want something else planted.

BANK ACCOUNTS

This is easy if you noted references in previous sections involving bill paying. Even if you have not added any co-signers to your bank accounts or ceded bill payment and record keeping to someone in anticipation of DDay, at the very least the information for your active bank accounts should be in the fireproof safe or safe deposit box you purchased earlier.

And if you went out to buy one you already know Herculean strength was involved to move that sucker to any reasonable place in your home. If someone helped you with the safe moving challenge you might leave them your gym membership.

You can also stick a label to the safe like my dad did saying: "No money or bearer negotiables in this box. Only policies, titles, registered documents, etc." That was too much information, but you get the idea. Most important, any old bank account documents should be destroyed along with the old locker and safe deposit keys addressed earlier.

Just because you are dead, and someone trusted has access to your information does not mean they can casually stroll into your bank and withdraw everything in your account and call it a day. This is the paper trail section after all. The Certified Death Certificate mentioned before is required as are other documents you thoughtfully left in your safe, lockbox, safety deposit box, or file cabinet.

The Document Checklist following the chapter on Contents of Safes includes a list of documents that your heirs need to carry around with them in a secure folder or submit via certified mail. Additionally, the bearer needs to have a picture ID, and be named as your heir or executor in trust documents or in your Will.

Your Social Security number will be requested frequently enough that your dutiful heirs will have it memorized, and an embossed birth certificate is helpful too. A property tax bill can be handy and add a utility bill with your address in the packet. Recent bank or account statements also have identifying numbers that are required.

If you are feeling very generous you can select a nice portfolio to give to the living saint whose future resume will include a year or more, as your personal clean-up butler. It is helpful for your butler to keep the basic requirements together in one secure and easily transportable bundle.

INSURANCE, ANNUITIES, AND IRAS

Insurance and annuities were sold to you years ago emphasizing their benefits to you like loans on value, and for your heirs as avoidance of poverty in case of your untimely death. While true on both accounts, there are negatives that you may or may not have become aware of in your lifetime.

To avoid the ire of institutions devoted to the sale of insurance and annuities and the investment of the money they received from such sales, I limit my comments to the minimum essential directives your family should understand.

Once you are dead, no one is in a hurry to pay off your heirs. There are myriad steps, trials, obstacles, and proofs that must be satisfied, possibly several times for the same account and to the same person before your clean-up crew receives any distribution.

The person attempting to collect these benefits should keep a calendar of contacts made with phone numbers, names of participants in phone calls, copies of documents sent, and as many notes as possible on what was said and to whom. If you think filing income taxes is difficult, this task is worse; but tax preparation provides an indication of what awaits your benefactors.

Even if they do everything perfectly, repeatedly, and with enough documentation to fill another file cabinet recently installed for your papers in an already overcrowded room bursting with your stuff, it is likely they will have to repeat the entire process multiple times with multiple entities. Maybe they will come to appreciate their hard-earned experience and can turn it into a business for other clean-up crew members?

IRAs are another thing entirely but are included here because the warnings and preparation are identical, with the added fun of decisions to be made about transfer of accounts or cash distribution with taxes paid. Traditional IRAs are savings vehicles and taxes are not paid until they are cashed out. Your inheritors either keep the transferred IRA and gradually pay taxes on received portions over time, or pay the taxes when the account is closed and all the value is taken. Taxes are paid regardless—of course.

Whoever you choose to handle this task is deserving of way more money than they receive from the closing of your estate so be really, really nice to that person if you haven't been already. Or maybe you are torturing them with this assignment?

I worked with a nice lady on the phone for what turned into ten months on an IRA of minimal value. There were institutional delays. Computer systems changed. There were waiting periods. Then she went on vacation. The company involved was a huge investment company but astonishingly had a tiny staff for such matters. She was the only employee who managed this (how is that even possible?). Think about it. Until the money leaves their care it is theirs to manage. What's the rush?

This essential woman went on vacation and broke both of her arms while playing ice hockey. True story. Her vacation turned into a convalescence and rehabilitation period. It became my fervent goal to wrap up this business before it rolled over into a new tax year. I did not want to file taxes for the deceased—again. She finally returned and we closed out the account. It was after Thanksgiving, but I got it done before the New Year. Mission accomplished. Barely.

You can make this easier for your crew by naming your inheritors specifically in your account documents or have a Living Trust drawn that addresses Annuities and IRAs specifically. When considering subjects for your haunting, annuities and IRAs offer ample opportunity.

TRUSTS, WILLS AND PROBATE

If you have enough wealth at the end of your days to have established trust accounts for those you leave, I wish you a hearty "Congratulations!" That also means you have a Will, so you are more prepared than most to move on to a less material world.

The date of the document is important in the movies, and it is also important in real life. Best to burn as you go and destroy out-of-date documents. It is also best if professionals have helped you with these documents and even better if they have copies stored in their vaults. I recommend keeping thumb drives, or whatever newfangled electronic storage system is hot these days, of the documents for you and your heirs, reducing tree killing and increasing the ease of home storage.

There are two potential areas of trouble with Trusts and Wills and neither of them is you, a well prepared dead person that you are or aspire to be.

The first is lawyers. Lawyers must be consulted, must be paid, and must do the work you hire them to do. And they have a schedule that is not your own. If you are in a hurry and feel like your breathing time is limited, ask around and get a lawyer who will come to your house or hospital room and consult with you.

This is a common situation and the legal profession can accommodate. Recommendations from friends, hospice workers, your church, the funeral home, and the internet are readily available. And if a lawyer arrives and you don't like them, feel free to boot them out. There are lots of lawyers. Don't call the one you spotted on the billboard while being transported to the hospital and be wary if your perpetually broke friend has a cut rate deal just for you.

And finally, you need to read the documents and understand them. That is part of the service you are paying for, so have someone you trust with you as back-up when the lawyer is explaining it all. If you no longer have someone you trust handy, then ask a representative of the organization that is the recipient of your estate to come and help. They have a vested interest in helping you get it right.

One of the primary reasons for consulting a lawyer regarding your estate and who gets what, is the potential for avoiding probate. Probate is not a dirty word, but it can take on that meaning as it often results in extended delays closing out your affairs and distributing any goodies you leave behind.

The process sounds worthy since the idea is that whoever is supposed to receive something gets what they are supposed to get and are who they say they are. But if your estate is complicated by people with claims on your valuables being already dead, sick, irresponsible, or angry, and if the value of what you leave is in dispute, it may be a blessing of sorts to have some official sort it all out in a maze-like administrative building with interminable phone menus.

Rules for when probate is required vary by locale so you need a lawyer to draw up a Trust or Will if there is any expectation of your heirs receiving what you want them to have without much delay and potentially avoiding probate.

The other thing a lawyer can help you consider is how much of a gift you can give your deserving team members before your DDay. It does not necessarily mean you cannot continue to use or enjoy whatever it is you want to eventually belong to someone else, but a lawyer is required to help make your final wishes come true. Think of your lawyer as your Magic Wand and make sure you trust your lawyer.

The second major difficulty with Trusts and Wills are the benefactors of your estate. Newspapers are filled with stories of affronted adult children suing their stepmother who is half their age for the "unfair" distribution of money that they had been counting on and possibly prematurely spending.

Even if your estate consists of the contents of your liquor cabinet and your cats to be cared for throughout their nine lives, people complain. If you leave money to the church or your favorite charity, your heirs may vehemently dispute the sanity of that bequest, or basically anything that excludes them.

There is nothing you can do at the end of your days to fix the conflict that has been stewing among your kin and hangers-on for generations. If there will be bickering, threats, and probable violence to come, all you can do is exactly what you want to do with as much preparation and legality as you can afford.

It is possible if people have an idea of what's

coming they may not react as badly as they might have done if surprised. If the neglect and exclusion they experience is no surprise, they may take it out on someone other than your cherished few. No guarantees, but false promises are sure to stir up a battle over very little and could result in more funerals over any amount of wealth.

WHERE YOU LIVE: REAL ESTATE

Where you live is important to a person regardless of their age or infirmity. Some people are not very attached to a place or to belongings. Others spend a lifetime building the nest of their dreams and their personal identity is firmly tied to it.

It is common for people younger than you to have strong opinions about where you should live, for how long, and what should happen to that place once you have left the building. Realizing that this section may reduce sales of this book or result in pages "accidentally" torn out, I suggest that if you pass for sound of mind, you may as well persist in following your own path, as so many of those with suggestions for you have insisted upon doing for themselves.

Elderly people have been moved out of their homes because "they might fall down, and no one will find them." Or because "they always have spots on their shirt and it's embarrassing." Or because "the place is filthy! I can't stand to be there!" I could go on, and on, and on.

People often have concerns for the elderly or aging person that have nothing to do with the feelings, needs, and opinions of the actual person in question. These types of concerns typically revolve around the feelings or worries of others, not the person under consideration.

If a pre-dead person living alone is frightened, lonely, or not ambulatory, help making choices about available options to be less fearful, more social or ensure more caretaking in a person's daily life is helpful and usually appreciated. If a pre-dead person is not frightened, enjoys privacy, and can manage the basics of life, although possibly not to the standards of others, then what?

If your family is hot on your tail to move you somewhere that you do not want to go, and you are as sound of mind as the rest of them and able to afford the choices you have made, then it is really up to you what you choose to do and how you want to live. It is not required that you move somewhere convenient for your extremely annoying sibling to visit.

There are no rules in life about how spotless your shirt must be. If you would rather fall down the stairs and die untended in your own home than move to a retirement home where you never see stairs again or hear the crickets out your back door either, that is also not against the law. May as well do what you want as long as you can and take care of Number One—You. Everybody wants that for themselves, but not necessarily for others.

Sometimes the older we become the more invisible we become, and the easier it is to be trampled under the fast and heavy feet of those around us. We may not be as feisty, energetic, and strong as we once were. What we can be in our older years is devoted to maintaining ourselves in the most authentic way possible. The opinions of the aged count. You can haunt them, after all.

You have been living somewhere. If it is in a retirement community where there is someone on a waiting list ready for your exit so they can step right up and move in, and your belongings move along with no trouble, then skip right over this section. If you have been renting and only your things and the landlord need to be dealt with, that is an easier prospect than if you have been in the family home of generations and there are five hundred acres and four hundred cows.

The more you have, the more likely it is that others are in a hurry to tell you what to do with it. It all comes down to the actual removal of your belongings and the sale of your house. The stuff of your life is dealt with in more detail in Part Three. Here the actual real estate consideration is discussed apart from the things that are inside the real estate.

If you own a condo, apartment, or home, the real property has value that your family may want to claim. The sooner the property can be vacated, cleaned, and possibly fumigated, the sooner real estate agents or lawyers can get involved and help your survivors decide how to market and sell your home. If you leave your house to someone, then it becomes their asset and is no longer the concern of the crowd waiting for their share of you. Clear disposition of your property is essential.

Documentation previously mentioned is a part of any transaction, so your paper trail comes into play. There are real estate agents and lawyers who specialize in estate home sales rather than relocation sales and that is the type of agent that is most useful. This is not the time to consult your brother-in-law's aunt who just got her real estate license even though she could really use the commission. If you need to hire an agent at all, then you need a professional in estate sales.

There may be security issues and neighborhood considerations, association rules and dues, house checks once no one is living in the home, mail, property tax bills, lawn maintenance, power outages, and threats of squatters. Once a house is empty, nothing good is likely to happen to it and many bad things may occur. Unless your heirs have people willing to keep an eye on all the mentioned issues and more, it is not a great idea to dawdle with the house sale.

My sister-in-law desperately wanted to stay in her home for the remainder of her days. She needed some assistance, and in the beginning, to prevent me from using all my money flying out to check on her and driving her batty in the process with my nurturing concern, we hired caregivers from a bonded company. This was during 2020, and you may remember a pandemic called COVID that limited human and social interaction.

Moving her into a facility may also have shortened her life and would mean no one outside the assisted living center could visit her for the foreseeable future. The caregivers we hired had schedules and supervisors, and even GPS trackers on the employees so the company knew where they were. By the way, if you have the means to pay for in-home caregivers, or if family and friends are able to handle this, it is a good idea to have their schedules alternate. That way Company A may catch oversights of Company B, and even if you cannot be there to see for yourself there will be many eyes to ensure the care that is given is the care you expect.

Hospice services are often provided in the home rather than in a dedicated Hospice Facility, and you and yours may be qualified for those services well before your DDay. Possibly years before. Hospice care givers are renowned for the miracles they perform, finding services you never dreamed of and exhibiting unimagined kindness. It is always worthwhile to check on eligibility for Hospice care.

My sister-in-law taught me many things during her years living at her home with regular caregivers. Some of the wonders of our modern world include phone apps for prepared food delivery, grocery delivery, household goods delivery, remote medical appointments, and video phone calls. I remotely ordered transportation for her and had medications delivered. I am now an expert on all of these things and more, thanks to her patiently allowing me to learn these skills as we came to need them. For a minimal fee, you can have a shopper go to the market of your choice and call you to consult on the ripeness of tomatoes or the brand of Cognac available.

There are pros and cons of every living situation at any stage of life and if in-home living is your plan you must think ahead to plan for the security of the home and autos, especially if there may be hospital or rehabilitation stays and there will be times the home is empty. In many nice expensive neighborhoods virtually no local residents leave anything in their cars. Doing so guarantees a break-in or car theft sometimes for something as small as spare change.

In some areas the threat of squatters helping themselves to an empty dwelling is a real danger and it can take a year or more and lots of money to evict illegal squatters, even if they have moved in for as little as one night. And what about the damage a crowd of rowdy teenagers can do if they party hard for a weekend? And who might be liable if one of them gets injured driving drunk on your Cognac while leaving your house you did not give them permission to use? You guessed it.

Local police will often assist with more frequent rides down your street if they are notified of your absence. Neighbors can be treasures keeping an eye on the house, watering the plants and feeding the cat. Wi-Fi camera security systems need not be expensive and can provide enormous peace of mind.

Many of the suggestions for security and caregiving when living independently are also solid ideas if you choose to live in a community of some kind; adult only dwellings, assisted living, hospice and nursing care. People may find themselves bored with provided food, wanting a visit with a rehomed pet, not seeing staff for help as often as needed, and suffering confusion with medical care. There comes a time in our lives, and it can come early or late in our stories, where our days will be happier if there are additional people looking out for us. The challenge for the elderly is that many of their favorite people have already had their DDay and are no longer available to help.

My friends and I have often discussed a widows' plan involving the joint purchase of an old-fashioned motel, sprawling, and all on one floor. We could each have our individual units with a shared area for meals, a bar, a coffee/tea center, and a smoking court for those who no longer care about the whiteness of their bonded uppers and plan to start smoking again when they reach ninety. If there's a pool, we may never risk getting into it but we may enjoy auditioning pool guys. Or a driver for us to call? I hope the self-driving car glitches are resolved soon, otherwise my husband may object to the interview process I have in mind for my driver.

We have yet to see our ideas in the marketing materials that flood mailboxes and emails of senior citizens. Exactly what kind of entertainment and dining do they provide and do we get a vote? The more options available that fit your needs, the greater your satisfaction will be with your home, and I say 'home' because that is what it is. Where you live is not a waiting room for your DDay, but your home.

I have posed the question repeatedly as to whether you will ultimately be a Ghost or Guardian to your people left behind. There is a real possibility you can inadvertently become your own Ghost, thoroughly missing Guardian potential, if you delay making choices about where you want to live if you face a future needing some care. I hope I have made it clear that frequently people younger than you have their own motives for evicting you from a home you find completely comfortable and appropriate. If you make your decisions and reinforce them with legality and arrangements you make yourself, you are better armed to forge your own path through the entirety of your life—a good plan regardless of age and infirmity.

Part Three deals with your stuff and how to handle it. As for your home, once a house is empty with no legitimate resident moving in, it is time for your clean-up crew to make the commitment to sell. A long empty house is a magnet for nothing good.

Part Three
YOUR STUFF
Instructions for Handling Earthly Belongings

When people start thinking about the end of their days or more likely, the days of someone else, the first things they usually think about are the things addressed in this section.

The Stuff. And it is typical to start with the biggest things first, the furniture, the clutter, the mess. It makes sense that we think this way because this is how we typically approach our own clutter, the dishes, the dust, the litter pans.

In a life that is being actively lived, that sort of clutter needs addressing first because it keeps on coming. The dishes keep piling up and the litter boxes keep filling up. In a life that is winding down or has come to a screeching halt, those things are not necessarily the highest priority because they are the easiest to deal with and the cleanup can often be outsourced, although that will cost money.

What follows is the guide for dealing with the Stuff of Life and it can be enlightening, heartbreaking, shocking, or dull. You can hand out assignments, but take care of what you can, while you can if Guardianship is your goal.

STUFF YOU MAY NOT WANT YOUR KIDS TO SEE

Think of diaries or old love letters to the wrong people. Journaling is "in" these days and many of us have the random journal lying around with entries from memorable trips, beautiful moments we want to hold on to forever that we haven't glanced at since putting pen to paper, and perhaps pages of complaints about our partner who may outlive us, detailing their annoying habits and passions.

Some journalists write regularly and fill pages with information and file the journals by date. This type of journal can be valuable to the living while they are living, and to those they leave behind as sources of information: the wonderful B&B you always booked, or your favorite oysters named for a tiny beach in Maine. If you are the latter type of journalist, your family already knows where you keep your journals and may check them to consult your life in print for information and entertainment.

The troublesome journal is the one tucked in the bedside drawer or in the back behind other books on a shelf that you may have forgotten existed. As you go through your home room by room, you should herd these journals into a corral out of view of impressionable witnesses and review their contents. Much of the corralled material should be sent to the locker (butcher), as we say in the Midwest, or for urbanites, to the shredder it goes. Composting these journals saves your survivors much irrelevant and potentially disturbing musing about your personal relationships and fantasies.

If you are more techie than pen and paper, you may use an e-journal and this record bears the same careful consideration discussed earlier. Do the contents merit saving for any purpose? Someone may figure out that impossible password one day, so if it has no value except to spur your memory, time to clear the memory banks and delete.

As always, you have choices. You can create an entirely fictional journal that epitomizes an exotic self, unimagined by your family. If you are wacky and wild already you can write a stodgy version for the fun of confusing everyone left behind. And if you have a box of journals people gave to you and you never got around to using, donate those so no one is disappointed to find their thoughtful gift neglected.

We all have a self-image we have developed

living our lives and yours may be messy, embarrassing, or confusing. Remember, you don't have the opportunity to explain yourself forever, so it is time for some hard choices. Are there photographs of you doing things you prefer to leave unseen? Take a good long look and let it go. Do your credit card statements reveal a life of living on the edge of solvency and good sense when you have lectured your children incessantly on the evils of such choices? Did you donate their college fund to Save the Whales resulting in your kid having a debt load they will carry for decades?

They don't have to ever know. Unless the big reveal is your goal, for good or evil.

STUFF YOU DON'T WANT ANYONE TO HAVE TO SORT THROUGH

This is typically the never-ending paper pile. Papers in the corner, papers in the filing cabinet, papers in boxes in the basement, or your collection of 126 Remy Martin glasses mixed up with fine crystal. For whatever reason, people often don't throw things out that are clearly trash. Even big things. Did you buy yourself a new desk chair and leave your old broken one in your office and now can't even see it because it is covered in junk mail you never got around to opening and magazines you never read?

Your post-life clean-up crew feels like they should go through all this in case there is something important in there, and if you want to torture them be sure to leave the car registration or some checks that may or not have been deposited among the debris.

STUFF OF VALUE THEY WILL ACCIDENTALLY TOSS IF YOU DON'T SORT IT OUT

You may know that the only existing baby pictures of your children are filed with your old check registers by the relevant year, but one look at the date on the box of canceled checks and out those photos may go. Do you buy coins of high value just in case the government runs the greenback into worthlessness? Costume jewelry is highly collectible and who knew those diamond earrings that were so huge you never wore them were real diamonds?

If you really don't care, that is up to you and maybe someone outliving you needs a new career selling on eBay, but if you hate to throw anything out because it might be worth something, it would be sad to avoid this task. And this is no time for regret. You could sell those diamonds yourself and have some fun.

STUFF OF VALUE YOU SHOULD SELL BECAUSE THEY DON'T CARE

It is hard to look at the stamp collection you have enjoyed for decades and know that your family considers it junk. It may be junk, or it may be valuable, but it is time to decide the future of such things. I speak from experience. Having closed the estates of four family members I have stared down their treasures and curiosities and have of course taken some of potential value into my personal storage bin, my home.

My father built a guitar using my Tinker Toys as braces and clamps when I was a small child. It is a beautiful thing, but not what a young guitarist is excited to pick up today. And my father had several old Martin guitars that are quite valuable. He loved guitars but that was a long time ago. Those instruments might be appreciated and used if I took them out of their filthy old cases and made some small effort to sell them.

I like and appreciate antiques myself so I think it's wonderful when I can have a piece of history in my home that is actually useful. But no one plays the guitar in my extended circle. I could go on vacation on that guitar. I should go, and soon. It may get lost or destroyed if I don't deal with it, and no one would feel good about that. And no one wants the Tinker Toy guitar even though he loved it and I do too. Maybe that can stay hanging on the wall as long as I can enjoy seeing it there.

Deal with such things while you can and enjoy your pre-dead years.

STUFF THEY WILL LOVE IF YOU ORGANIZE IT NOW

This is the part where you must get out of your bathrobe and get to work! Organize the work like anything you do well, with plans, vision boards, and deadlines. Or lock yourself in a room with the pile and don't feed yourself until it is done. Or maybe until it is started? This is work for sure, and it may lead you down memory lane, messily sobbing all over the papers and stuff you are trying to organize.

I have cassette tapes that my family members sent around from one to the other when my father was stationed in Vietnam as an Air Force officer. I have tried to listen to them, and the sound of the voices knocks me flat. And the fragility of the tapes makes me nervous. What I need is professional help and soon; or possibly a capable friend and a bottle of scotch or two. There are many ways to approach a problem, but the work absolutely needs to be done.

Think of photos, family videos, recordings, and keepsakes people have admired over the years. Jump into this activity before no one knows who the people are in the photographs and some crafty person turns them into greeting cards. I know someone who gave up on family VHS recordings and made a coffee table out of them. I don't know if they could be pried apart and digitized or not, or if this is a family archive that is ready for burial with the owner.

This type of thing is the most fragile and treasured part of the legacy we leave behind and unless you kept the baby books up to date and day-by-day from your first child to your eleventh, I suspect you have a pile of work to do. Me too.

Did we exist if we leave no curated record? Did we leave the legacy we meant to leave, or a mess of neglect as if we didn't value the life we lived? I want to make mine count and I hope you do too.

STUFF THEY CAN DO, NO PROBLEM— LEAVE IT TO THEM AND DON'T WASTE A MINUTE ON IT.

Ironically, this is the stuff people see first when looking at clearing out a home and think it is the biggest challenge because it takes up the most space. The good news is that this is the easiest stuff to deal with, by far.

Clothes and soft goods—Clothes can go to consignment centers if you have the time to take the trouble but be sure to use one where you get cash back rather than credit for shopping. And clothes can be donated. My mother had a closet full of business suits I donated to an organization helping women get back into the workforce. Linens can go to donation boxes or animal shelters to be cut up and used in kennels. If you don't already have this habit, take up emptying your pockets. One pocket full of folding money is a minor curse. All of your pockets filled with change, gold fillings, and the occasional large uncashed check is a nightmare for someone that should be deliberate.

Furniture and household goods. The bad news about what is known these days as "brown" furniture, is that the beautiful cherry dining room table you saved and scrimped for is likely worth very little in resale. If you can give it or will it to someone who wants it, do that first. You can have yard sales or auctions, and neither is easy or particularly profitable, but circumstances vary. Some towns and neighborhoods have special events you can leverage and get rid of loads of belongings in a single weekend. There are buying services who come to the house and pay cash for the things that interest them. The fine furniture you are sitting on while they look around will fetch less than the box of collectible knick knacks, but at least they will pay you rather than you paying them to take it all away.

There are companies in most areas that clean out houses to the bare bones and make the stuff disappear. They resell what they can, then donate and dump the rest. They are typically amazing, speedy, and inexpensive, and once they are on the case there is no going back. The things your team thought they could sort through until their own DDay will be irretrievably gone.

You can rent a dumpster. My husband loves the dumpster but prefers my stuff tossed into it rather than his. One night I caught him climbing into the dumpster to retrieve an old COCO computer that had resided in a box in the attic for twenty years.

A dumpster of appropriate size is a good idea when preparing for any move, saving hours of effort schlepping things, and backaches and trips to the ER. You are preparing for a permanent move, so consider a dumpster. At the very least it gets the attention of your family, friends, and neighbors. The neighbors will be annoying with questions about your health in anticipation of getting a steal of a deal on your house, but you are setting a great example for them and their own ultimate cleanup. Be sure to ask them about their own backache and blood pressure. You are not the only one on a timer!

There are cleaning companies that do empty house cleaning too, and the cost of this is worth every penny compared to the physical and emotional cost of your family dealing with the dust of days long gone. Leave a jar with cash for this in the back of the fridge and it buys you major kudos on Earth, and in Heaven or wherever you may go.

Part Four
SPECIAL WARNINGS

STUFF THAT DOESN'T BELONG TO YOU

It could be a case of forgetfulness, or it could be grand theft, but if you have a trove of belongings that do not belong in your house, move those things along right away. If you are embarrassed about the chainsaw you borrowed from your neighbor and denied to his face that you still had, either sneak it into his tool shed or donate it—maybe in the next county.

Don't worry about the library books. Dump them in the return box or leave them to the living to return. But if you have a shed full of all the neighborhood bicycles that ran over your gardens, see if you can discreetly relocate them or return them to their original owners. Odds are you won't get the returns right even if you try, so leave one in every driveway and stay alive long enough to watch what happens.

If the items that you find in your house are a complete mystery to you and you have no idea where they came from, and you hope your cousin is not using your basement as storage for stolen goods, make it known you are cleaning house in a serious way and threaten the arriving dumpster as the likely destination. Then go ahead and relax or die, worry free.

DANGERS OF STORAGE UNITS

Storage units remote from your home are a recent phenomenon. Before personal commercial storage facilities, people were forced to either live among their belongings, sell them, or give them away. Young couples refinished their parents' furniture and wore hand-me-down clothing that came from an attic instead of a consignment shop. I have an older friend with a large family who stores jeans in her attic organized by size. Jeans are the only clothing she considers worth passing along.

Stories in the news of hoarders perishing in an avalanche of their own stuff, and houses filled with cats and dogs who eventually dine on their deceased master, are warning tales, but they can't have anything to do with us, right?! Those people had real problems, nothing like the millions of us who spend tens of thousands of dollars storing things of dubious value conveniently out of sight.

The commercial storage unit is an easy solution when a person dies and there is an entire household of stuff to manage. They are especially attractive with the infamous offer of $1 for the first month. Loved ones advise survivors to be gentle and take care of themselves and store everything until they stop crying unexpectedly and are ready to face the looming task of really dealing with it all.

That may be kindness, or it may be a secret way to get revenge for a forgotten but horrific slight. What real kindness looks like is a genuine offer to visit on a regular basis with wine, garbage bags, and a large car, and the energy to help. If you can't yet be forced into the actual work, a cocktail hour where you make plans for the actual work is a good first step. Real friends should not let friends fall into the storage pit.

My personal experience was painful and expensive. My parents died leaving a house full of stuff. My brother took their car and a brass tray, and headed back to L.A. His ties to our parents were sincere but not tethered by much stuff. Eventually we sold the house and there was pressure to empty it quickly.

There were clothes, tools, dishes, furniture, photos, records, guitars and computers. They left their house with all the goods and items that fill a home. There were packed boxes of things they had not unpacked from their last move, time capsules of a sort. There were linens, plants, and an unruly cat. There were foodstuffs, appliances, and full file cabinets.

There were genealogy records and old family letters, makeup and cleaning supplies. To say I was overwhelmed does not begin to cover it. Many of these belongings seemed to contain the essence of my parents like vapors in the air.

When possible, I placed the items, like an adoption, with someone who needed them and was excited about them, and in those cases I parted with the things gladly. If they had no willing takers and might be orphaned in the world, they went instead to a storage unit.

I kept two large storage units for two years. If I needed a tool or detergent, I stopped by the storage unit and looked around before I went shopping. My children checked them out occasionally but were properly fearful of the piles of dusty boxes filled with inaccessible stuff. They were undoubtedly afraid that I would die before I got rid of it all.

When my daughter got married, she asked me

for wedding photos of parents, grandparents, and great grandparents to display around the reception area. Such a lovely and sentimental request from a dear thoughtful daughter. Guess where those photos were? In the storage units.

It is part of my belief in a greater power that the day when I finally got the nerve to head into the dim light of the storage units, the family photographs were safe at the top of a pile in an accessible box. If I had disappointed my daughter on her wedding day because of piles of dusty, neglected things, I would have cursed myself with eternal regret.

It may surprise you to know there is a society in storage facilities. You will get to know your storage unit neighbors. Occasionally, I met someone and caught a glimpse of their stuff in the gloom. A few times (only a few, honest!) I even bought a bunch of stuff from someone and moved it directly from their storage unit into mine. I can hardly believe it myself. See how dangerous this is?

Eventually I was forced out of my storage pit by nature and diminishing funds. I arrived at the facility one day to find a note stuck on the door informing me that I should check for water damage in my units. The stuff that was unsorted and neglected may have been damaged by a broken pipe.

I could have been paying for years to store what could overnight have become a pile of moldy, damp trash, rather than the vaporous essence of my parents. I thought about what my father might say about all this and was immediately my six-year-old self again, not in charge of my own life.

I began to work in the units, sometimes alone, but often with the help of friends to keep me company, bring me lunch, and make me leave before I was completely chilled and asthmatic. I cleaned out enough that what remained did not need to find a family member for adoption or perpetual care.

I sent evites and had a series of parties in the units. I served wine, coffee and brunchy food and used battery operated aroma lights to improve the sketchy ambiance. I supplied boxes and bags, and the rules were that guests could take whatever they wanted, but they also had to take something away they did not want.

They could put it in the trash at their home, take it to a donation center, anywhere that was not my garage. Where, you guessed it, I already had all the stuff from the storage units that I still had to identify, sort or deposit with another family member.

The good part of this saga is that as I visit my friends now, I am often reminded of my parents. The dry sink that sits in the corner, the bookshelf at the top of the stairs, or the bed I sleep on when I visit. The bad part is the extended self-torture and small fortune I contributed to the storage unit industry.

The only safe storage unit is the one that sits in your driveway and is large and unsightly. Eventually your neighbors make enough comments, and the passing dogs will mark it sufficiently that you must get rid of it.

There was a movie some years ago about Pod People who placed their Pods all over the Earth to take over our world. It has already been done and we have succumbed. I believe there is always hope, and resistance is not futile. Unless you plan to live in a storage unit—do not rent a remote storage unit.

Last Notes to the Pre-Dead
If you complete even a fraction of the things recommended in this book you will not only meet your reward as prescribed by your belief system, but you will have hymns of praise sung in your name after your passing. Your children will go among their peers, speaking with gratitude for your amazing foresight and compassion. Your assets will find their way to places of your choosing, and new curse words will be associated with those who failed to follow the directives in this book—not you! You will be a Guardian Angel rather than an Evil Specter or Ghost of Clutter Past.

You will still be dead, and I am unclear if that is good or bad since I am still living myself. This is not a book on immortality, but directions on how to avoid infamy. Good luck! Pax Vobiscum and Auf Wiedersehen. We will all end this journey on Earth. Let those we leave behind have no cause to curse us when we are gone.

DISCLAIMER

This is not a legal reference of any kind and should not be construed as a judgement on any individual living or dead or any industry or business either fictitious or real. There are many practical and softer spoken books available on this subject. Have you read them yet? I thought not.

This book is a kick in the pants to get going on preparation no one wants to ponder. There will be rewards. I promise.

ACKNOWLEDGEMENTS

This book could not have been written without dear family and friends, living and departed, who generously trusted me in their lives and in their deaths. My parents, Virginia and Wood, my brother Tomme and his dear partner Sharon, and of course my children Aaron and Regan who I hope will count me as a Guardian one day, a very long time from now!

We have all gone through our losses together, most recently my son-in-law Jeff whom I hope I have supported warmly. I am also grateful for the C.L.I.M.B and Brave Women at Work retreat I was invited to attend by my daughter-in-law,

Stephanie, with the request to bring something I have written that I was willing to share.

The women at that event encouraged me and gave me the confidence to climb out of the file cabinet and share something that can help others. My husband Bruce has tolerated my various enthusiasms for years but always said he hoped he would one day be married to an author. I hope he was thinking of me!

Special appreciation goes to my friends from my New Jersey book club with whom I have read broadly for forty-two years. I hope you enjoy my contribution to the material.

ABOUT THE AUTHOR

Cyndy Wulfsberg was born in Texas and has lived in six states, one territory, and two foreign countries. Early travels with her Air Force family inspired lifelong interest in languages and cultures.

Physical challenges lead to a love of dance and commitment to whole body wellness.

She holds a B.A from Luther College in Political Science, and an M.A in Sociology from the University of Virginia. Her career spans university teaching, elected public office, consulting, lobbying, and national and international marketing and sales.

As one of the youngest of her family she has served as executor for four family members and knows that hard things are easier with a dose of humor.

She is devoted to her family and friends and lives in Michigan with her husband, cats and bees.